7 Seven Wonders

Seven Wonders of
ANCIENT GREECE

Michael Woods and Mary B. Woods

TWENTY-FIRST CENTURY BOOKS

Minneapolis

To Matthew Woods

Twenty-First Century Books
A division of Lerner Publishing Group, Inc.
241 First Avenue North
Minneapolis, MN 55401 U.S.A.

Website address: www.lernerbooks.com

Library of Congress Cataloging-in-Publication Data

Woods, Michael, 1946–
    Seven wonders of ancient Greece / by Michael Woods and Mary B. Woods.
        p.   cm. – (Seven wonders)
    Includes bibliographical references and index.
    ISBN 978–0–8225–7574–0 (lib. bdg. : alk. paper)
        1. Greece—Antiquities—Juvenile literature. 2. Greece—To 146 B.C. –Juvenile literature. I. Woods, Mary B. (Mary Boyle), 1946–
    II. Title. III. Title: 7 wonders of ancient Greece.
    DF77.W66 2009
    938–dc22   2007051033

Manufactured in the United States of America
1 2 3 4 5 6 – DP – 14 13 12 11 10 09

Contents

INTRODUCTION

*P*EOPLE LOVE TO MAKE LISTS OF THE BIGGEST AND THE BEST. ALMOST 2,500 YEARS AGO, A GREEK WRITER NAMED HERODOTUS (ca. 484–425 B.C.) MADE A LIST OF THE MOST AWESOME THINGS EVER BUILT BY PEOPLE. THE LIST INCLUDED BUILDINGS, STATUES, AND OTHER OBJECTS THAT WERE LARGE, WONDROUS, AND IMPRESSIVE. OTHER WRITERS ADDED THEIR OWN IDEAS TO THE LIST. THE WRITERS EVENTUALLY AGREED ON A FINAL LIST. IT WAS CALLED THE SEVEN WONDERS OF THE ANCIENT WORLD. THE ANCIENT WONDERS WERE:

THE GREAT PYRAMID AT GIZA: *a tomb for an ancient Egyptian king. The pyramid still stands in Giza, Egypt.*

THE COLOSSUS OF RHODES: *a giant statue of Helios, the Greek sun god. The statue stood in Rhodes, an island in the Aegean Sea.*

THE LIGHTHOUSE OF ALEXANDRIA: *an enormous beacon to sailors at sea. It stood in the harbor at Alexandria, Egypt.*

THE HANGING GARDENS OF BABYLON: *magnificent gardens near the ancient city of Babylon (near modern-day Baghdad, Iraq).*

THE MAUSOLEUM AT HALICARNASSUS: *a marble tomb for a ruler in the Persian Empire. It was located in the ancient city of Halicarnasssus (in modern Turkey).*

THE STATUE OF ZEUS AT OLYMPIA: *a statue honoring the king of the Greek gods. It stood in Olympia, Greece.*

THE TEMPLE OF ARTEMIS AT EPHESUS: *a temple honoring a Greek goddess. It stood on the coast of the Aegean Sea, in modern-day Turkey.*

Most of these ancient wonders are no longer standing. Wars, earthquakes, weather, and the passage of time destroyed them.

Over the years, people made other lists of wonders. They listed wonders of the modern world and wonders of the natural world. Some even listed wonders for each continent and many countries. This book is about the wonders of ancient Greece.

A WONDERFUL PLACE

Greece is part of the Balkan Peninsula in southeastern Europe. To the east is the Aegean Sea, and to the south and west is the Mediterranean Sea. The country is made up of the Greek mainland and many islands. Mountains, rivers, farms, vineyards, and olive groves fill the landscape.

This beautiful land is home to one of the world's oldest civilizations. Civilizations are organized societies. They have governments, cities, roads, writing systems, art and culture, science, a steady food supply, and armies to protect themselves.

Greek civilization is more than five thousand years old. The ancient Greeks have given many gifts to the world. For example, the Greeks formed the idea of a democracy, a type of government in which ordinary people vote their rulers in and out of power. Almost 65 percent of the world's nations, including the United States, enjoy some form of democracy. The ancient Greeks also left their unique mark on art, theater, architecture (the design of buildings), philosophy (thoughts, beliefs, and learning), and many other fields— even sports!

A TRIP BACK IN TIME

Get ready to visit some of the wonders of ancient Greece. *Ancient* is another word for "old"—so we will explore cities, temples, monuments, and other wonders from long ago. One stop will be a mysterious spot where people gathered to hear the voice of the Greek god Apollo. We will also stop at the site where the Olympic Games were first played—almost three thousand years ago. Other stops will include an ancient medical center and a city that legend says was built by one-eyed giants. Get ready for adventure—and some surprises—as you set off on your tour of ancient Greece.

Knossos

The ruins of the palace of King Minos on Knossos, a Greek island, show the remnants of large columns and stairways.

 NCIENT GREEKS LOVED MYTHS AND
LEGENDS ABOUT GODS, GODDESSES, MONSTERS, SUPERVILLAINS, AND
SUPERHEROES. ONE STORY TOLD OF KING MINOS, WHO LIVED IN A
GREAT PALACE ON KNOSSOS. KNOSSOS IS A GREEK ISLAND SOUTHEAST
OF MAINLAND GREECE. THE PALACE AT KNOSSOS HAD A LABYRINTH, A
MAZE OF ROOMS AND PASSAGEWAYS. ONCE SOMEONE WAS INSIDE THE
LABYRINTH, HE OR SHE COULD NOT FIND A WAY OUT.

According to myth, the Minotaur lived deep inside the maze. The
Minotaur was a terrible monster—half human and half bull. To keep the
monster happy, Minos began feeding it humans. Minos forced the king of
Athens (a Greek city) to send him seven boys and girls every nine years.
When the Athenian youths arrived in Knossos, Minos locked them in the
labyrinth. There, the Minotaur found and ate the youths.

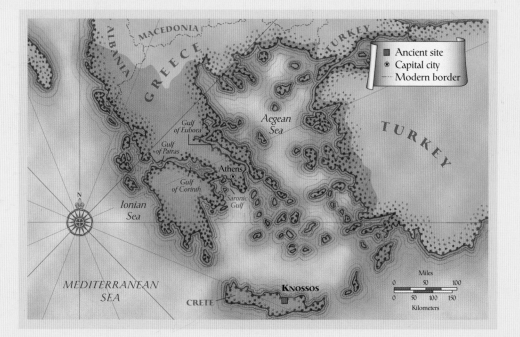

Theseus, a young Athenian prince, could not stand watching his own people being sent to their death. He vowed to go to Crete and pretend to be one of the seven male sacrifices. Once inside the labyrinth, he would kill the Minotaur.

King Minos had a daughter, Ariadne. Ariadne saw Theseus as he arrived in Knossos. She fell in love with the handsome prince. Thinking he was an Athenian sacrifice, she decided to save him. As Theseus was headed into the labyrinth, Ariadne gave him a ball of thread. As Theseus walked through the maze, he unraveled the thread behind him. Theseus met the Minotaur, and the two fought a fierce battle. Theseus finally killed the monster and followed the thread backward to escape from the labyrinth.

Theseus slays the Minotaur in this illustration by Henry Matthew Brock from a book on Greek tales published in 1928.

PASS IT ALONG

People in modern times thought that Knossos was just an imaginary place—that it had never really existed. But in 1878, a Cretan merchant named Minos Kalokairinos discovered some ancient ruins at Knossos. Kalokairinos's discovery drew the interest of archaeologists—scientists who study buildings, tools, and other remains of ancient civilizations. In 1900 a British archaeologist, Sir Arthur Evans arrived at Knossos. He started excavations—the digging up of buried ruins.

Evans did not find the labyrinth or the skeleton of the Minotaur. But he

"There is a land called Crete in the middle of the wine-blue water, a handsome country. . . . There are ninety cities. . . . And there is Knossos, the great city, the place where Minos was king."

—The Odyssey, *a Greek poem created by Homer in the 800s B.C.*

discovered something almost as fantastic. He found an enormous building that seemed to be the ruins of King Minos's palace. Knossos proved to be part of a previously unknown ancient civilization. Historians named it the Minoan civilization after King Minos.

The discovery of Knossos showed that the Minoans actually were the first western civilization in Europe. Archaeologists realized that civilization in the region was hundreds of years older than anyone thought. Minoan culture flourished on Crete from about 2900 to 1200 B.C.

Left: *British archaeologist Sir Arthur Evans started excavating the palace at Knossos in 1900.* Below: *Evans also reconstructed parts of the palace, such as this part of the north entrance.*

Minoans were great sailors and traders. They sailed to ancient Egypt in Africa and saw how the ancient Egyptian people lived. The Minoans might have adopted some parts of ancient Egyptian culture—traditions, customs, and arts—and brought them back to Knossos.

ANCIENT TOILETS

As excavations went on, Evans realized how amazing the Knossos palace was. It was as big as five high school football fields. It had more than 1,300 rooms connected by hallways, passageways, stairways, and doors.

Minoan palaces were almost like entire towns under one roof. Rooms for the royal family made up only a small part of the building. Knossos had rooms for hundreds of other people to sleep and eat. It had stores that sold food and other goods. Workshops for stone carvers and pottery makers lined the passageways. Storerooms stood filled with grain, cooking oil, and other food.

The palace had a central courtyard about 165 feet (50 m) long and 82 feet (25 m) wide. People might have gathered in this open area to enjoy the fresh

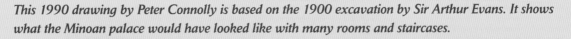
This 1990 drawing by Peter Connolly is based on the 1900 excavation by Sir Arthur Evans. It shows what the Minoan palace would have looked like with many rooms and staircases.

air, hold markets, and socialize. Streets connected the courtyard with the rest of the palace.

Knossos was built on different levels, with stairways leading to each floor. Small courtyards opened to the sky to let in light. Pipes made from baked clay pottery brought freshwater into the palace. There were bathrooms with pools of water for bathing. One bathroom had what might have been the world's first flush toilet. This toilet was a seat over a drainpipe that emptied outside the room. Minoans "flushed" it by pouring in water from a jug.

Who lived in this great palace? We do not know for certain. Perhaps it was the residence of King Minos and other Minoan royal families and their servants. Archaeologists think that a large community of more than 80,000 people lived on land surrounding the palace.

SEALSTONES TELL STORIES

Knossos was not built all at once. It was built over time between 1700 and 1400 B.C. Minoan rulers probably enlarged it as the population grew. Builders used a soft stone cut from nearby quarries (places where stone is dug or cut from the ground). The stone walls got a coat of smooth plaster. Some of the rooms were decorated with frescoes—colorful wall paintings showing scenes from everyday life in Knossos.

Frescoes and paintings on pottery vases and pots are among the few sources of information we have about the ancient Minoan civilization. The Minoans did have a written language. It is called Linear A, because the writing was in straight lines. But modern researchers have not been able to translate Linear A. No one knows the language on which it was based.

We know a little about the Minoans from sealstones. Sealstones are small pieces of stone carved with dolphins, octopuses, and other designs. When the stone was pressed into soft wax or wet clay, it left an image of the design. The

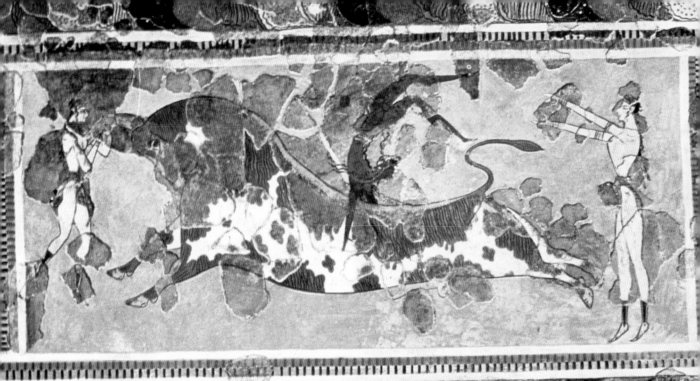

This restored wall painting from the palace at Knossos shows acrobats jumping over a bull. It was found in a vestibule (entry room) of the palace.

seals probably were placed on letters, bills, and other documents much like we use rubber stamps.

The designs on sealstones tell archaeologists about the Minoans. For example, all the fish and other aquatic designs show that the Minoans were great sailors.

Where seals have been found also tells us something. Documents and other items with Minoan seals have been found in Greece, Turkey, and other Mediterranean countries. This tells archaeologists that the Minoans traveled to, did business with, and traded culture (such as art) with other countries.

LET'S PLAY
Leapbull!

In leapfrog, one player gets down on his hands and knees and another leaps over his back. Young Minoan boys and girls played leap*bull*—which was a little more dangerous. In bull leaping, players ran directly at a charging bull. Minoans grabbed the bull's sharp, pointed horns; leaped over the head; and landed on its back. Then they jumped off and tried to escape before the angry bull could turn and spear them with its horns.

THE DECLINE OF MINOAN CIVILIZATION

Minoan civilization declined during the 1400s B.C. But without written records, we do not know why. Archaeologists can tell from the ruins that fire destroyed Minoan palaces and their surrounding communities on Crete. But they do not know what caused the fires. It might have been earthquakes or wars.

Some archaeologists think that the Minoans got into battles and wars with the Mycenaean people. The Mycenaeans were building their civilization on the Greek mainland. They took over Crete in 1450 B.C. The Mycenaeans rebuilt Knossos and occupied the palace and other Minoan land. Knossos was later destroyed again by another fire.

A MODERN WONDER

Evans did more than uncover and study the ruins at Knossos. He restored and rebuilt part of the palace in the way he thought it once looked. The rebuilt palace still is there. Almost one million tourists visit Knossos each year to see that reconstruction and marvel at its size.

Archaeologists from many different countries are still studying the ruins at Knossos. They are trying to discover whether there was any truth to the myths about this ancient kingdom. Archaeologists also want to know how the city was built and how its people lived. But archaeologists worry that large numbers of tourists may damage artifacts (such as statues, tools, and weapons) that could provide that information.

Tourists study the wall paintings on part of a restored wall at the palace at Knossos.

2 Mycenae

The ruins at Mycenae are visible in this modern-day image of the top of the mountain.

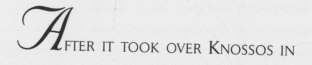

*A*FTER IT TOOK OVER KNOSSOS IN 1450 B.C., MYCENAEAN CIVILIZATION CONTINUED TO GROW. IT BECAME THE MOST POWERFUL FORCE IN THE REGION SURROUNDING THE AEGEAN SEA. MAINLAND GREECE WAS DOTTED WITH MYCENAEAN CITY-STATES. CITY-STATES WERE CITIES THAT EACH HAD THEIR OWN RULERS, LAWS, AND ARMIES.

The city-state of Mycenae sat in the mountains of a Greek region called the Peloponnese. The city was fortified—protected by high walls and guarded gates. A watchtower perched on a nearby mountaintop.

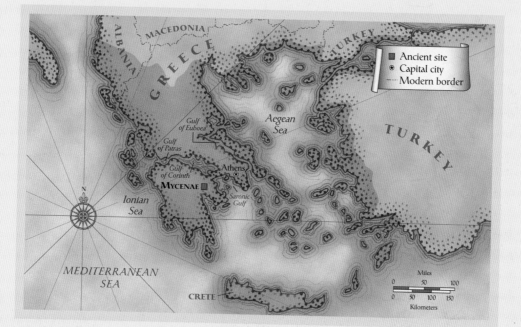

This modern photo shows the Lion Gate, the main entrance to Mycenae. Two lions are carved in stone above the entrance.

A visitor to ancient Mycenae would climb up the hills from the seacoast. A long stone walkway led around the fortress. On each side of the walkway, the visitor would be dwarfed by cyclopean stone walls. Some of the walls were 36 feet (11 meters) high. They were called cyclopean because of their size. Legend says that the walls were so big that they must have been built by a race of giants, the cyclopes.

At the end of the walkway, the visitor would pass under the main gate, the Lion Gate. The gate was topped by a carved stone relief of two lions more than 10 feet (3 m) tall. Inside the gate and past the guardhouses, the visitor would find a busy city. The streets were filled with temples, markets, workshops, and homes. And in the midst of it all was the royal palace.

"The wall, which is the only part of the ruins still remaining, is a work of the Cyclopes . . . , each stone being so big that a pair of mules could not move the smallest from its place to the slightest degree."

—*Pausanias, who wrote about Mycenae, ca. A.D. 150*

CITY OF THE *Cyclopes*

Later Greeks could not imagine how normal workers could move the stones at Mycenae. They came up with the explanation that a crew of cyclopes came to Mycenae to build the walls. According to Greek myth, a cyclops was a giant with a single eye in the middle of its forehead.

Parts of Mycenae's walls were about 25 feet (8 m) thick and more than 30 feet (9 m) high. That's about the height of a three-story building. Some of the blocks used to build the walls weighed as much as a modern car. The blocks near the Lion Gate weigh at least 20 tons (18 metric tons) each, almost as much as two school buses. We still do not know how ancient people cut, moved, or lifted those blocks without modern tools or machines.

AGAMEMNON AND THE TROJAN WAR

Many of the city-states farmed and traded their food and goods with neighbors. But they also often fought one another. Wars were one way to gain wealth. If a city was conquered, the winner could take home all its riches and sell its people as slaves. Piracy was another way to gain wealth and power. Some of the city-states, including Mycenae, robbed the ships that sailed the Aegean and Mediterranean seas.

Over time, Mycenae became one of the most powerful Greek city-states. It rose to the height of its power in the 1200s B.C. At that time, Mycenae was ruled by a royal family called the Atreids. Agamemnon was probably the most famous Atreid. He was king when Mycenae led a huge army of Greek kings and soldiers against the city of Troy (in modern-day Turkey). The attack became known as the Trojan War.

Agamemnon and the Greeks won the Trojan War. They destroyed Troy and stole all its gold and jewels. Agamemnon returned to Mycenae more powerful than ever. But his rule did not last long. Legend says he was killed by his wife soon after returning.

The end of Agamemnon and the Atreids echoed the end of Mycenaean civilization. Historians believe that by 1100 B.C., most of the city-states had been destroyed, including Mycenae. They might have been destroyed by an invasion of people from the north, the Dorians. Greece was plunged into a dark age in which people struggled just to make a living. There was no time for great cities, art or literature, or trade with other countries.

Greece overcame its dark age in the 800s B.C. But Mycenae never recovered. For a while, its ruins were an ancient tourist attraction. Travelers from Athens came to see what was left of the cyclopean walls, the Lion Gate, and some beehive-shaped buildings they called treasuries. Eventually, though, the great city became a tumble of stones hidden in the high windy hills.

HOMER'S TALES

Mycenae might have been lost. But Agamemnon and the Trojan War lived on in history through stories told for centuries. For a long period in history, the Greeks did not write down their literature. Instead, they recited stories again and again as poems. One of Greece's most popular poets was Homer. Homer created, memorized, and recited very long poems about the Trojan War.

Eventually, about 800 B.C., Homer's followers wrote down his Trojan War stories as *The Iliad* and *The Odyssey*. *The Iliad* tells the story of one year of the Trojan War and a fight between Agamemnon and another Greek hero named Achilles. *The Odyssey* is about the adventures of soldiers returning home after the war.

The Iliad and *The Odyssey* became great works of literature, read by people all over the world. But by modern times, some scholars had begun to doubt that the Trojan War had ever really happened. They thought Agamemnon, Achilles, and other heroes were made-up characters. No one could find any trace of Troy. And looking at the ruins of Mycenae, scholars thought stories about the great city must have been exaggerated.

HEINRICH SCHLIEMANN

Not everyone doubted Homer's tales about the time before Greece's dark age. Heinrich Schliemann (1822–1890) first read about Agamemnon and the Trojan War in the 1830s when he was growing up in

German archaeologist Heinrich Schliemann, shown here in 1875, searched for the city of Mycenae.

This image from 1900 shows the graves inside the city of Mycenae that Schliemann excavated.

Germany. As an adult, Schliemann became a very wealthy businessperson. He retired early and decided to devote himself to archaeology.

In the 1870s, Schliemann began a search for evidence of the Trojan War. He wanted to prove that the cities and people Homer wrote about had been real. He spent many years searching for the ruins of Troy, using *The Iliad* as a guide. Schliemann then began searching for Agamemnon's city, Mycenae.

WONDROUS DEATH MASK

Schliemann and his team (including his wife, Sophia) arrived in Mycenae in 1876. They dug through many feet of dirt and stone just to get into the ruined city. Outside the cyclopean walls, they worked on digging out the doorways of the treasuries. Inside the walls, they uncovered traces of the city's layout.

But Schliemann was eager to find gold and beautiful artwork. He was disappointed at how slow and difficult the digging was. He was almost ready to give up when Sophia noticed something in the dirt. She and Schliemann bent down and began to dig more carefully. They had discovered the top of a shaft grave. A shaft grave is a tomb, like a small room, dug into bedrock.

> *"I have gazed on the face of Agamemnon!"*
> —*Heinrich Schliemann's message to the king of Greece*
> *after opening a grave in Mycenae in 1876*

The Schliemanns and their team discovered several of these shaft graves clustered together. At first, they dug up incredible jewels, coins, dazzling golden cups, and decorative weapons. Then they discovered eighteen bodies buried in the graves. Time and the weight of the earth covering the graves had destroyed some of the bodies. But some were so well preserved that they looked almost like mummies.

The men buried in the shaft graves had masks over their faces. Each mask was made of gold hammered so thin that it could be molded to the shape of the wearer's face. Schliemann could tell from the masks what the person had looked like while still alive. He was particularly struck by one mask showing a handsome, middle-aged man. Schliemann was convinced that he was looking at the death mask of Agamemnon.

Schliemann thought he had discovered further proof that the ancient stories about Troy and Mycenae were true. Archaeologists later realized that Schliemann had his time periods wrong. The graves at Mycenae were from an era before the Trojan War. They dated back to the 1600s B.C. The "treasuries" outside the city walls were more likely the burial place of Agamemnon and his followers. It was found that these buildings were not really treasuries once filled with gold. They were royal tombs. Archaeologists date the tombs back to the 1200s B.C.—the time of the Trojan War.

City of Wonders

Schliemann was wrong about his dates. He was too eager to find evidence of the Trojan War and jumped to conclusions. But his work helped archaeologists realize that Mycenae was not just a mountain fortress ruled by robber-kings. The archaeologists examined many artifacts—weapons, tools, jewelry, and pottery—found at Mycenae. They saw that the city and its people were much more advanced than anyone had thought.

Schliemann and those who came after him found jewelry and pottery from eastern Europe, the Middle East, and Egypt. They found art and building decorations that matched cities in other parts of Greece.

Above: *This is the entrance to one of the tombs outside the walls at Mycenae.* Below left: *This mask is the one Schliemann believed covered the face of Agamemnon.* Below right: *This piece of Mycenaean pottery from the 1200s B.C. shows Greek warriors armed with spears.*

They found items made purely for enjoyment, such as jewelry and delicate pottery. They found evidence of religious ceremonies. All this told the archaeologists that the people of Mycenae traded ideas and goods with other civilizations. They were interested in other cultures and in developing their own culture.

Archaeologists and historians began to understand a new period in ancient Greek history. They began calling the people of this period the Mycenaean civilization after Agamemnon's walled city.

Information about Mycenae is important. It was the first civilization on the Greek mainland. Some historians say the Mycenaean people were the first Greek people. The Mycenae people developed the culture adopted by all the other people who later lived in Greece.

A MODERN WONDER

Mycenae became famous as one of the places where European civilization began. Tourists began to visit the ancient ruins while Schliemann was still working there. Ever since, Mycenae has remained a popular site to visit. The massive Lion

BURIED IN *Beehives*

Early rulers and other important people in Mycenae were buried in shaft graves. These box-shaped tombs were dug in the ground and lined with slabs of stone. Later on, important Mycenaeans were buried in "beehive tombs" *(below).* They were called that because they look like dome-shaped beehives. These huge chambers were dug into hillsides. Their sloping sides were lined with blocks of stone. The most famous beehive tomb, built at Mycenae around 1350 B.C., is called the Treasury of Atreus. Atreus was Agamemnon's father. The treasury burial chamber is 43 feet (13 m) high and 14.5 feet (4.4 m) across. Two stone slabs at the entrance each weigh 100 tons (90 metric tons).

This modern image shows the ruins at Mycenae lit up at night, with the Lion Gate in the foreground. The lights from the Greek city of Argos can be seen in the distance.

Gate has been restored. Tourists can see ruins of palaces and temples. They can almost imagine the cyclopes lifting up huge blocks to build Mycenae's walls.

In an effort to preserve this wonder for future generations, the United Nations Educational, Scientific, and Cultural Organization (UNESCO) selected Mycenae as a World Heritage Site in 1999. These buildings, monuments, and other places are an important part of human history. In receiving this honor, the government of Greece agreed to establish a plan for protecting the ruins at Mycenae.

3 Epidaurus

The ancient theater at Epidaurus is shown in this modern image. The Greek theater is still in use in the twenty-first century.

*W*HEN PEOPLE IN ANCIENT GREECE GOT SICK, THEY DID NOT GO TO A DOCTOR'S OFFICE, EMERGENCY ROOM, OR HOSPITAL. IN THOSE DAYS, THE KIND OF MEDICAL CARE WE ARE USED TO DID NOT EXIST. INSTEAD, PATIENTS WENT TO TEMPLES DEDICATED TO ASCLEPIUS, THE GREEK GOD OF HEALING.

The temples were called Asclepions. People believed they could discover how to cure their illness by sleeping in Asclepions. The most famous Asclepion in ancient Greece was near Epidaurus, a small town southwest of Athens.

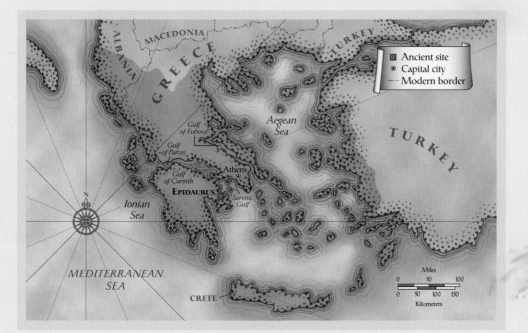

Patients hoped that while they slept in the Asclepion, Asclepius would appear in their dreams. He would tell them how to get better. The temples also had priest-healers called the Asclepiadae. Asclepiadae gave patients medicines made from plants and flowers. They also gave advice about how to live in healthier ways.

The Asclepion at Epidaurus was also called the Sanctuary of Asclepius. Sanctuaries were centers of religious worship. They had temples, altars, and statues honoring the gods. The sanctuary at Epidaurus opened in the 700s B.C. It continued to attract patients until the A.D. 500s. During those 1,200 years, people from around the ancient world came to Epidaurus for medical help.

FAMOUS DOCTOR

Asclepius probably was a real person, a very good doctor who treated people in Greece in about 1200 B.C. Ancient stories say that Asclepius could cure almost any illness. People told stories about Asclepius's skill, and some of the stories grew exaggerated. One story said Asclepius brought dead people back to life.

What makes us think that Asclepius *(below)* might have been a real doctor? In *The Iliad*, the famous story about the Trojan War, Homer mentions a man named Asclepius several times. Homer mentions that Asclepius's sons were great healers. Some historians believe that *The Iliad* might have been about real people and a real war. So they believe Homer might have been talking about a real doctor when he mentions Asclepius.

"*As a surgeon, Asclepius became so skilled in his profession that he not only saved lives, but even revived the dead.*"

—*Apollodorus, a Greek scholar who lived in the 100s B.C.*

After Asclepius died, legends and myths turned Asclepius into the god of healing. Sick people prayed to Asclepius and got better. They might have gotten better anyway, but they gave Asclepius the credit. The worship of Asclepius spread from Greece to ancient Rome and continued into the A.D. 600s.

Sick people also worshipped two of Asclepius's daughters, Hygeia and Panacea, as goddesses of health. From their names, we get the modern words *hygiene* (cleanliness to stay healthy) and *panacea* (a medicine that cures all illnesses).

The ruins at Epidaurus show the remains of the circular, domed structure called a tholos.

Ancient legend said that Asclepius's staff, or walking stick, had a snake coiled around it. That's how a staff with a coiled snake became the modern symbol of medicine in some countries. We call it the staff of Asclepius. In some countries, a staff with two coiled snakes is the symbol of medicine.

FOR GOODNESS SNAKES!

Some ancient Greek treatments involved superstition (a belief that goes against common sense) and magic. One idea, for instance, was that snakes could cure certain diseases. One kind of snake was allowed to slither through the temple-hospitals at Epidaurus and other places. It became known as the Aesculapian snake. Aesculapian snakes were big—some grew to 6 feet (2 m) long. But the snakes were not poisonous. Later, this creature was renamed the rat snake because its diet includes rats.

Rat snakes would slither through the temple-hospitals as patients slept. They flicked patients with a forked tongue. Snakes smell with their tongues, and the Aesculapian serpents were just trying to sniff out a tasty meal. But ancient Greeks thought that the tongue's touch could cure diseases, infected sores, and cuts.

HIPPOCRATES

Priest-physicians also treated diseases with natural remedies and cures. They kept the recipes and knowledge of these cures a secret. The secrets were passed from father to son, generation after generation.

One ancient Greek physician, Hippocrates (460–380 B.C.), wrote down those secrets. Hippocrates threw out treatments based on magic and superstition. He separated medicine from religion and taught that every disease had a natural cause.

THE *Hippocratic Oath*

Hippocrates *(above)* became known as the father of medicine. Hippocrates wrote an oath (a serious promise) to be taken by new doctors as they begin practicing medicine. In part, the ancient Hippocratic oath reads, "I swear by Apollo, Asclepius, Hygeia, and Panacea, and I take to witness all the gods, all the goddesses, to keep according to my ability and my judgment, the following Oath." In modern times, many new doctors still take an updated form of the Hippocratic oath. They promise to practice good medicine in the best interests of their patients.

Our modern medical treatments are based on that ancient idea. Epidaurus and other sanctuaries helped people develop modern ways of preventing and treating diseases. The world's first medical schools, for instance, were built at temples dedicated to Asclepius.

THEATER OF WHISPERS

Epidaurus became so famous that some people traveled for weeks to reach this great healing center. Patients brought gifts of gold, silver, and jewels for the gods and priest-physicians. Epidaurus had treasury buildings to hold the gifts. Since people stayed in Epidaurus while being treated, the town needed other buildings. It had a hotel, restaurants, baths, a building for people to exercise, and places of entertainment.

People in ancient Greece loved to watch actors perform plays on a stage in theaters. A very famous theater was built at Epidaurus in the 300s B.C. This huge building looked like a sports stadium without a roof or dome. Almost 14,000 people could sit in the open air in the moonlight and watch actors perform on the stage.

Above: *The ancient theater at Epidaurus is still used in the twenty-first century. Performances are put on for locals and tourists visiting the ruins.* Below: *This drawing shows what the temples and sanctuaries at Epidaurus may have looked like.*

Usually in a big theater, it is difficult for people in the back rows to hear voices from the stage. That's why modern theaters have microphones and loudspeakers. In those days, however, there were no microphones. How did those big audiences *hear* the actors?

The theater at Epidaurus was built in a special way. People in the back row could hear the faintest whisper spoken on the stage. Modern scientists have studied this amazing feature. They think it results from the rows of limestone seats and walls. The stone amplifies (makes louder) sounds from the stage. It also filters out the murmur of the crowd in the seats.

This reconstructed part of the Sanctuary of Asclepius dates back to 360–350 B.C. It is located at the museum at Epidaurus.

A MODERN WONDER

In 1988 UNESCO placed Epidaurus on its list of World Heritage Sites. These places must be preserved because they are an important part of world history. Epidaurus continues to be a wonder for crowds of tourists who visit each year.

Many of the buildings at Epidaurus now are in ruins. They are surrounded by fences. Visitors can look but are forbidden to touch the ruins. Some of the artifacts are on display in a museum located on the grounds. Epidaurus's famous theater, however, has been restored and reopened. In the summer, people attend plays and other performances and can still hear every whisper on the stage.

4 The Oracle
AT DELPHI

A view of the ruins of the Temple of Apollo and the theater at Delphi. The theater is built up the hill from the Temple of Apollo and looks out over the temple and the valley below.

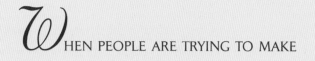

*W*HEN PEOPLE ARE TRYING TO MAKE AN IMPORTANT DECISION, THEY OFTEN ASK FOR ADVICE. CHILDREN AND TEENAGERS MAY ASK THEIR PARENTS FOR HELP. TEACHERS, GUIDANCE COUNSELORS, CLERGY, BROTHERS OR SISTERS, AND FRIENDS CAN ALSO GIVE ADVICE. SOME PEOPLE SEND QUESTIONS TO NEWSPAPER AND INTERNET ADVICE COLUMNS SUCH AS DEAR ABBY. OTHERS CALL ADVISERS ON RADIO TALK SHOWS.

In ancient times, people probably asked relatives and friends for simple advice. But for more important questions, they consulted people called oracles. The word *oracle* also referred to a temple or place in which a human oracle could be found. The most famous oracle in the ancient world was at the city of Delphi on the slopes of Mount Parnassus in southern Greece.

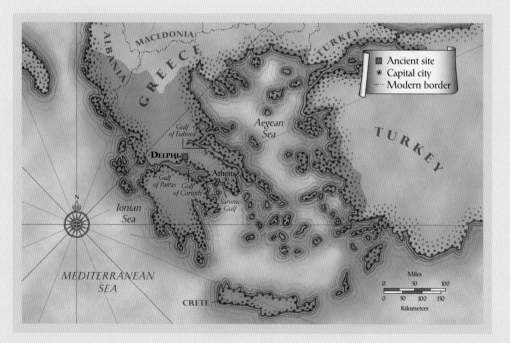

The ancients believed that oracles provided wisdom straight from the gods. Everyone thought that oracles got answers from the gods and passed them along to humans. Since the gods could see the future and never made mistakes, an oracle's advice was very valuable.

For almost one thousand years, people from Greece and other countries journeyed to Delphi to get guidance from the oracle. They thought that the oracle of Delphi got information from Apollo. Apollo was one of the most important ancient Greek gods. He was the god of prophecy (predicting the future), healing, light, poetry, and music.

Kings, generals, and other leaders came to Delphi for advice on whether they could defeat enemies in wars. Wealthy people asked the oracle whether they should marry a particular person. Priests came for divine guidance on when to hold religious festivals or where to build temples. Farmers wanted to know the best time to plant crops.

THE ORACLES NEVER ERRED

The Greeks believed that the oracle always spoke the truth. If things did not turn out as the oracles predicted, it was because people misunderstood the advice. Quite often, the oracles did give very vague answers. These answers could have different meanings. Picking the wrong meaning could be disastrous.

A man named Croesus learned that lesson the hard way. In the 500s B.C., Croesus was the king of Lydia, a land that became part of modern Turkey.

Croesus (second from right), the last king of Lydia, is shown in this fifteenth-century illustration by Robinet Testard. The artwork was published in a manuscript by French author Jean de Meun.

Lydia was at war with the Persian Empire, a great kingdom centered in southwestern Asia. In 546 B.C., Croesus planned to cross the Halys River in Asia Minor (part of modern-day Turkey) to attack the Persian leader Cyrus the Great. But before he went into battle, Croesus went to Delphi.

Croesus asked the oracle if he would win a war against the mighty Cyrus. The oracle told Croesus that after crossing the Halys, he would destroy a great empire. Feeling confident, Croesus attacked the Persian Empire and was defeated. The oracle was correct. Croesus did destroy an empire—*his own.*

EVER *Wonder?*

What makes us think that ancient writers were right about the oracle's secret? Ancient stories said the oracles at Delphi got their inspiration by breathing in a gas released from a hole in the ground. Modern scientists have discovered that a gas does leak from the ground at Delphi. It is ethylene, which has the sweet smell mentioned by ancient writers. This gas also puts people into a dreamlike state in which they think they see visions of the future.

APOLLO'S TEMPLE

No one knows exactly when or how Delphi became the ancient world's center for advice and prophecy. One story says that it began about 800 B.C. with a goat herder. The herder noticed that one of his goats had fallen into a hole in the ground. The goat was making strange sounds and grinding its teeth. When the herder climbed into the hole to rescue the goat, he had visions of gods and saw events that would happen in the future.

"It is a fact that the room in which they seat those who would consult the god is filled . . . from time to time with a delightful fragrance coming on a current of air which bears it towards the worshippers. . . . It is like the odor which the most exquisite and costly perfumes send forth."
—*Plutarch (ca. A.D. 46–120), a Greek historian, on the oracle at Delphi*

This painting from the nineteenth century shows a priestess sharing the wisdom from Apollo at the temple.

A group of priests who worshipped Apollo built a temple around the hole. They thought that Apollo was sending messages to people through the hole. The priests selected women to sit near the hole to pass Apollo's wisdom on to other people. These women were called the Pythia, named after the python (large snake) from one of Apollo's legends. There might have been several Pythia who took turns working at the temple and being the Oracle of Delphi. When one died, a new Pythia was chosen as a replacement.

OPEN FOR BUSINESS

Delphi worked like a modern business. The oracle opened for business on the seventh day of each month during the spring, summer, and autumn. People had to pay for advice. Common people lined up with goats, sheep, or other goods to pay the oracle's fee. Wealthy people, who paid in gold or silver, went to the front of the line. Before consulting the oracle, people also had to buy a sacred cake, which was very expensive, as an offering to Apollo.

The oracle sat on a chair in a temple. The floor had a hole right over the hole where the goat fell. Stories say that a sweet-smelling gas rose out of the hole. The Pythia inhaled the gas, saw visions of the future, and answered the person's question. Sometimes the Pythia gave an answer that could be understood. Other times, she just babbled and priests interpreted her words.

As Delphi's fame spread, more and more people came for advice. Delphi grew from a tiny village to a fabulous town. It had temples and other buildings filled with beautifully carved marble statues and other works of art.

Above: *The ruins of the Temple of Apollo are visible in this modern photo. The temple* (also shown below) *dates back to the fourth century* B.C.

In addition to the Temple of Apollo, archaeologists have found ruins of other temples, a theater, and a stadium. There also were treasury buildings where the priests kept the gold and silver.

After traveling for weeks to reach Delphi, many people probably stayed for a while. They had to wait in line to consult the oracle. They also might have wanted to rest before starting the journey back home. There must have been hotels, shops, restaurants, and other buildings to provide for the visitors. Cultural events, such as plays, and sports events also were held at Delphi.

THE ORACLE AND THE *Olympics*

Every four years, athletes gathered at Delphi for a famous athletic competition called the Pythian Games. They were named for the Pythia, the women who took turns acting as the oracle. Those games led to the Olympic Games, which started in Olympia, Greece, in 776 B.C.

The ruins of a stadium at Delphi date back to 500–400 B.C. The Pythian Games were held every four years at Delphi.

Above: *This carving was found in a treasury at Delphi and is from 525 B.C. It is now in the Delphi Museum in Greece.* **Left:** *This rock face at Delphi is where people left offerings for Apollo when they sought advice from the oracle.*

RUNNING OUT OF GAS

Archaeologists estimate that hundreds of thousands of people came to Delphi over the years. Delphi attracted some of the most important people in the ancient world, including kings, queens, and generals. By bringing together people from different cultures, Delphi influenced the way other ancient cultures developed.

For example, people from Greece and Rome met and got to know one another at Delphi. They shared ideas about laws, art, and other ways of living that helped shape ancient civilizations. People took those ideas back home.

Many of Delphi's sculptures and artistic treasures disappeared after Rome conquered Greece in 146 B.C. Roman emperors took hundreds of Delphi's most beautiful statues and other works of art to Rome.

The theater at Delphi can seat five thousand spectators.

By the A.D. 300s, fewer and fewer people were coming to Delphi for advice. Some historians think the people lost faith in oracles over the years. Others think that the gas that gave the Pythia their visions ran out. Then, in A.D. 390, the Roman emperor Theodosius decided that people should not worship gods such as Apollo. He ordered that Delphi and other shrines be closed.

A MODERN WONDER

Since 1987 Delphi has been on UNESCO's list of World Heritage Sites. Visitors to Delphi can still see ruins of some of this wonder's most famous buildings. Each year almost one million people climb the stairs up Delphi's slopes to see the temple of Apollo, the ancient theater, treasuries, and other buildings. Some even stand silently and ask for advice. A new archaeological museum, the Delphi Museum, displays important ancient Greek artifacts found at Delphi.

The Delphi site also includes the ruins of the Sanctuary of Athena (a Greek goddess). The ruins are about a half mile (1 kilometer) from the main ruins at Delphi. They date back to 380–360 B.C.

5 Olympia AND THE OLYMPIC GAMES

The altar of Zeus can be seen at the ruins at Olympia. Olympia is where the first Olympic Games were held in 776 B.C.

$\mathcal{E}$VERY FOUR YEARS, BILLIONS OF PEOPLE WATCH THE WORLD'S MOST FAMOUS SPORTS EVENT, THE SUMMER OLYMPIC GAMES. ATHLETES SELECTED FOR THE OLYMPICS GATHER IN ONE CITY AND COMPETE FOR CHAMPIONSHIPS IN DIFFERENT SPORTS. THE OLYMPICS ARE SO IMPORTANT THAT THE HOST CITIES START PREPARING YEARS IN ADVANCE. WHILE BEIJING, CHINA, WAS GETTING READY FOR THE 2008 OLYMPICS, FOR INSTANCE, LONDON, ENGLAND, WAS ALREADY PLANNING THE 2012 OLYMPICS.

This modern sports wonder began in 776 B.C. in the ancient town of Olympia, Greece. Cities from all over the Greek world sent their best athletes to Olympia to compete in footraces, boxing, wrestling, discus, javelin, long jump, horse and chariot races, and other events.

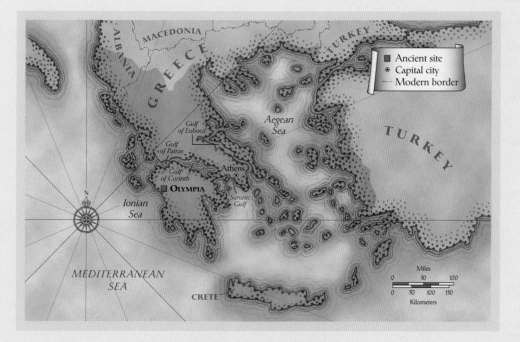

In those days, Greece was not one country. Instead, Greece was still a land of city-states with their own rulers, laws, and armies. These city-states often were at war with one another. But during the Olympic Games, city-states across the land agreed to a truce, or a period of peace. It allowed athletes and spectators to travel safely to and from Olympia.

ANCIENT SPORTS NUTS

Several stories explain how the Olympics began. One legend says that Zeus, king of the ancient Greek gods, started the Olympics. Zeus wanted to celebrate after winning control of the world. But in truth, the Olympics were started by ordinary people. Ancient Greeks loved sports, were great athletes, and often held competitions.

Those games served as entertainment and as a way for the Greeks to honor

Runners are shown on this pottery from ancient Greece. This vase is on display at a museum in Great Britain.

EVER *Wonder?*

How do we know that there were strict rules in the first Olympics? Pausanias wrote about the rules in the A.D. 100s. Pausanias said athletes and their trainers had to swear an oath that they would obey the rules while competing in the Olympics. The judges also had to promise to make fair decisions about who won each Olympic event.

This image from the 500s B.C. shows a Greek athlete throwing a discus.

their gods. Sporting events were held at many religious ceremonies—even funeral services where dead people were buried. The ancient writer Homer described one funeral that included boxing, wrestling matches, discus throwing, and footraces.

Someone eventually came up with the idea of inviting the best local athletes to compete for titles in various sporting events. The Olympics were one of four famous athletic competitions called the Panhellenic Games. *Panhellenic* means "of all Greeks." The Panhellenic Games drew athletes from all over Greece and were held in different parts of the country.

While the Olympics honored Zeus, the Pythian Games at Delphi honored Apollo. The Nemean Games, held near the town of Nemea, honored Zeus. The Isthmian Games, held near Corinth, honored Poseidon (the

"And we compel [urge] men to exercise their bodies not only for the games, so that they can win the prizes—for very few of them go to them—but to gain a greater good from it for the whole city, and for the men themselves."

—*Lucian Anacharsis, a Roman writer, ca. A.D. 170*

Greek god of the sea). The games took place in a four-year cycle called the Olympiad.

The festival at Olympia became the most famous. Olympia already was one of the most important religious spots in Greece. It was the perfect place for a national athletic event honoring the gods. Olympia had other advantages, as well. It was easy to reach by ship, for instance. That was important because athletes and spectators came from faraway places (such as Spain and Egypt, where Greece had established colonies). It would have been difficult for them to travel because they came by foot or horse and wagon.

In addition to sports competitions, there were races with horses and chariots and competitions for soldiers. Statues of athletes who won Olympic events were built at Olympia. When winners returned home, their neighbors treated them like sports superstars and celebrities. People in the town were happy because the victory made their city famous throughout Greece. Athletes got front-row seats at the theatre and free meals in restaurants. Some cities built new homes or gyms for their Olympic stars.

AMAZING *Athlete*

Milo of Croton *(below)* was one of the most famous ancient Olympic athletes. He won the wrestling championship in five straight Olympics. Stories say that Milo amazed people with demonstrations of his great strength. Milo held out a hand with the fingers spread, for instance, and challenged people to bend his little finger. Nobody could do it. Milo started training for the Olympics by carrying a newborn calf on his shoulders each day until it became a fully grown cow.

WONDROUS SITE

The Temple of Zeus was the most famous building in ancient Olympia. Completed in about 456 B.C., it was one of the largest temples in Greece. People went to the temple to worship a gigantic statue of Zeus, which was almost 40 feet (12 m) high. Made of ivory and gold, the statue was one of the original Seven Wonders of the Ancient World. Other beautiful sculptures of athletes, athletic events, and chariot races lined the inside of the temple.

Below: *This modern image shows one of the remaining columns of the Temple of Zeus at Olympia.* **Left:** *This color engraving of a statue of Zeus at Olympia came from a nineteenth-century German collection.*

"Many are the sights to be seen in Greece, and many are the wonders to be heard. But nothing does Heaven bestow more care than on . . . the Olympic Games."

—*Pausanias, an ancient Greek writer in the A.D. 100s*

Several other temples were built at Olympia, including the Temple of Hera (a Greek goddess and Zeus's wife). The modern Olympic flame has been lit at this temple since 1936. The flame is used to light a torch that runners carry to light a flame in the city where the next Olympic Games are being held.

Ancient Olympia had many other buildings. There were places for the athletes to live, train, and bathe. The Hippodrome was a huge track for horse and chariot racing. The rulers of city-states brought gold and other gifts for the gods. These valuable items were stored in treasury buildings at Olympia.

THE GAMES END

The Olympic Games continued for 1,170 years. But in A.D. 426, the Roman emperor Theodosius stopped the Olympics. In the A.D. 500s, terrible floods from two nearby rivers buried Olympia in a layer of mud more than 21 feet (7 m) thick. In the following centuries, many of Olympia's buildings were damaged or destroyed. People gradually forgot about this ancient wonder.

In 1766 an English archaeologist named Richard Chandler rediscovered Olympia. German archaeologists began excavating and uncovering the buildings in 1829. Olympia became a historic site.

The games that began in Olympia were started again in 1896. That was the first modern Olympic competition. It was held in Athens, Greece.

A MODERN WONDER

The Olympic Games have made Olympia one of the most popular places for tourists to visit in Greece. Olympia became even more famous in 1989, when UNESCO named it a World Heritage Site.

Only the ruins of most buildings remain at the site. But the nearby Olympia Museum contains many artifacts from the excavations. The artifacts include a famous statue of Nike, the Greek goddess of victory. Legends say Nike, a winged goddess, flew down from the sky to hand palm leaves to the Olympic victors.

Above: *These remaining columns at Olympia were once the palaestra, where wrestlers and boxers trained for the Olympics.* Below: *These columns are what is left of the Temple of Hera at Olympia.*

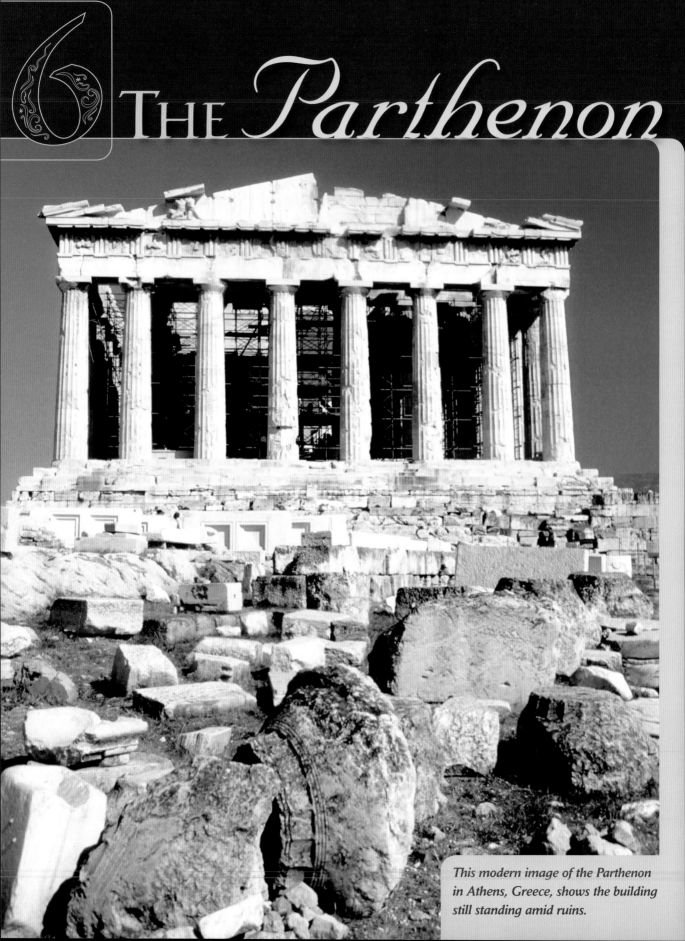

6 THE *Parthenon*

This modern image of the Parthenon in Athens, Greece, shows the building still standing amid ruins.

ONE ANCIENT GREEK BUILDING IN ATHENS HAS BECOME THE SYMBOL FOR MORE PLACES AND IDEAS THAN ALMOST ANY OTHER BUILDING IN THE WORLD. THE PARTHENON, BUILT IN THE 440S B.C., IS THE SYMBOL OF THE CITY OF ATHENS, ANCIENT GREECE, AND THE MODERN COUNTRY OF GREECE. PEOPLE AROUND THE WORLD ALSO RECOGNIZE THE PARTHENON AS A SYMBOL FOR CIVILIZATION ITSELF.

When countries of the world that are members of the United Nations wanted a symbol of culture and education, they chose the Parthenon. It became the symbol of UNESCO, which, among other things, encourages and supports education.

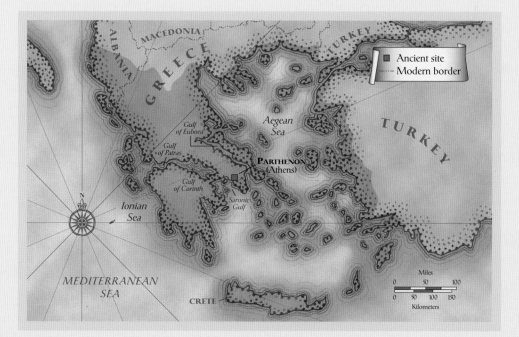

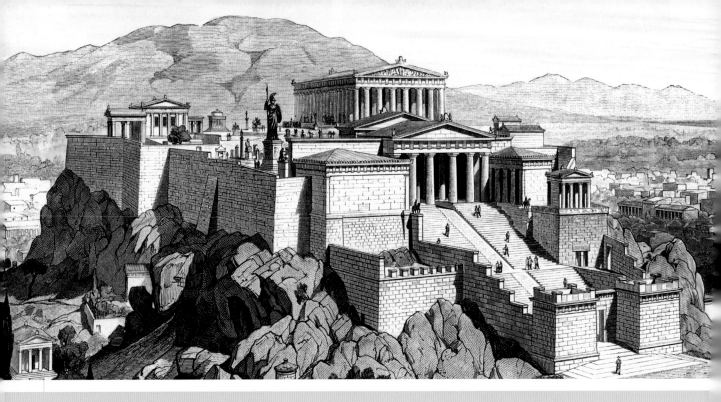

This woodcut shows the Parthenon and a statue of Athena atop the Acropolis in ancient Athens. The woodcut is from an 1882 book about Greece and Rome by Jakob von Falke.

Pictures of the Parthenon also make people think of European civilization (which began in ancient Greece) and the kind of government that started in Greece. That government is democracy, in which citizens or their elected representatives rule. In a democratic country, a majority of the people decide how everyone will live. In some other kinds of government, everyone must obey one ruler who thinks he or she knows best.

WORLD'S MOST PERFECT BUILDING?

Some people say the Parthenon is the world's most perfect building. It has graceful marble columns and beautiful statues. And the Parthenon seems to have proportions—length, width, and height—that are perfectly balanced.

However, it is only one of several ancient Greek masterpieces on the Acropolis. The Acropolis is a natural showcase—a high, flat hill that towers over Athens. Temples on the Acropolis were built for worship of ancient Greek gods. People living down below in Athens could see the Acropolis temples and pray to the gods. The temples have awed and amazed people for more than one thousand years.

EVER *Wonder?*

What did the Parthenon look like when it was new? A full-scale replica of the Parthenon was built in Nashville, Tennessee. Nashville calls itself the Athens of the South. Built in 1897 as part of a World's Fair in Nashville, the replica serves as an art museum in the center of a large public park. In 1982 Nashville's Parthenon added a replica of the statue of Athena Parthenos. It stands almost 42 feet (13 m) tall.

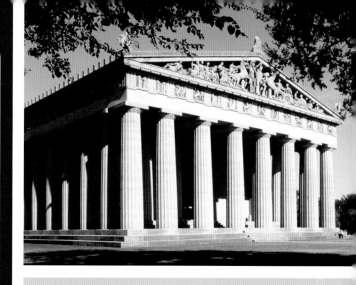

Above: *This replica of the Parthenon was built in Nashville, Tennessee, in 1897.* Below: *This modern image shows the Parthenon's many columns. Many modern architects think the building has a perfectly balanced design.*

This modern photograph shows the Acropolis in Athens with the city below. Visitors to the site can still view the ruins of the temples up above them on the hill.

Many other ancient cities had an acropolis, which means "the high city." It was often the highest and safest place in town. Cities needed an acropolis to protect the residents from enemies. When an enemy army attacked, residents could flee to the acropolis for protection.

The Acropolis in Athens is the world's most famous high city. It rises about 500 feet (150 m) high and covers an area about as large as eight football fields. From the top, people could see the surrounding countryside—and approaching enemy armies—from far away. The Acropolis was easy to defend, since enemies had to march uphill and climb over a wall. The Acropolis also had wells with plenty of water for people to drink while surrounded by enemy armies.

On this safe haven, the ancient Greeks put their most sacred and most important buildings. Those buildings were temples to the gods, where people could pray for victory over their enemies. Temples also were treasury buildings for safeguarding the city's gold and other valuables.

BUILDING THE TEMPLES

The people of Athens built temples on the Acropolis in the 500s B.C. But Persian armies destroyed the temples during a war with Athens in the 480s B.C. The Greeks eventually defeated the Persians and built new temples on the Acropolis later in the 400s B.C.

A great leader of Athens named Pericles convinced the Greek people to build those temples. Pericles put four magnificent buildings on the Acropolis— the Parthenon, the Propylaea, the Erechtheion, and the Temple of Athena Nike. The largest of these was the Parthenon. It was built as a temple for Athena, Zeus's daughter and the Greek goddess of wisdom and war. Athena was the patron, or guardian, of Athens, and the city was named for her.

"The statue of Athena . . . carries a statue of Nike about 4 cubits [6 feet, or 1.8 m] high, and a silver spear in the other hand. A shield is placed by her feet, and near the shield is a serpent."

—*Pausanias, who visited the Acropolis and saw the Parthenon, ca. A.D. 160*

The Propylaea, built from 437 to 432 B.C., was the entrance to the Acropolis. The Erechtheion was built in 420 B.C. for worship of Athena, Poseidon, and Erechtheus (a legendary king of Athens). The Temple of Athena Nike was built in about 427 B.C. Athena Nike is a version of Athena that shows her as the goddess of victory.

Planning for the Parthenon began in 447 B.C. The building and statues were finished by 432 B.C. The Parthenon was built as a rectangle, 98 feet (30 m) wide and 226 feet (69 m) long. Each end has eight columns. Each side has fifteen. The columns are more than 34 feet (10 m) high. The columns are carved in the Doric style (named after the Dorians). Doric columns are thicker, shorter, and plainer than other types of Greek columns.

Sitting atop the columns is an area called the entablature. The entablature is a band between the columns and the base of the roof. The Parthenon's entablature is carved in great detail. It has two parts—the triglyphs and the metopes. The triglyphs are square pieces with three columns carved in relief (standing out from the surface).

In between each triglyph is a metope. The metopes are also square pieces carved in relief. The Parthenon had ninety-two metopes. The carvings feature scenes from Greek myth and history. For example, some metopes show a battle between Greeks and centaurs (mythological creatures that are half human and half horse).

The Erechtheion temple has caryatids. These statues are sculpted female figures that serve as columns, or support beams, for a building. The name comes from the Greek word karyatide, *which means "maidens of Karyai," a town in ancient Greece. These kinds of statues were also found at Delphi.*

On each end of the Parthenon, under the peaks of the roof, are triangles called pediments. Like the metopes, the pediments were decorated with relief sculptures. The pediment sculptures also show scenes from Greek myth, including the birth of Athena. In Greek myth, Athena sprang fully grown from Zeus's head—wearing armor and carrying a spear!

The Parthenon represents "the supreme effort of genius in pursuit of beauty."

—*Auguste Choisy, a French historian who studied the Parthenon in the late 1800s*

Inside the temple's outer columns, near the ceiling, is a frieze. A frieze is a horizontal band that is painted or carved. Visitors to the Parthenon could follow its 525-foot (160 m) frieze around the temple, watching as the carved pictures unfolded a story. The pictures show horseback riders, humans, gods and goddesses, musicians, and animals during a Greek festival.

Inside the Parthenon were twenty-three more columns stacked in two stories. At the far end of the main room was a huge gold, silver, and ivory statue of Athena. Known as Athena Parthenos, she held a smaller statue of Nike in her hand. In Greek temples, the statues of gods and goddesses faced the doorway. Athena Parthenos watched the carved bronze doors of the Parthenon across a shimmering reflecting pool.

THE ELGIN MARBLES

Over the centuries, the Parthenon has suffered serious damage. In the A.D. 600s, it was converted into a Christian church. Church leaders did not want images of Greek gods on their church, so they removed many metopes and sculptures. In the 1400s, Greece was taken over by the Ottoman Empire, a Muslim government centered in Turkey. The Parthenon was then used as a mosque (Islamic place of worship).

The Ottoman army later stored bombs and weapons in the building. In 1687 those bombs were ignited during a battle with the city-state of Venice (Italy). The explosion blew away the Parthenon's roof and shattered its insides.

In 1801 the Earl of Elgin, a British official in Greece, got permission from the Ottomans to remove many of the temple's remaining sculptures. He shipped them

ANCIENT Piggy Bank

Rulers of Athens turned Athena Parthenos into the city's bank account. They gave her a dress coated with 2,500 pounds (1134 kg) of gold. When the city needed money, the gold was removed and used to buy weapons and other goods. The statue was damaged by several fires, and we do not know what happened to the remains.

These stone carvings of horseback riders are part of the collection known as the Elgin Marbles. The marbles were removed from the Parthenon in the early 1800s and shipped to London, England.

to the British Museum in London, England, where they went on display. Those marble statues became known as the Elgin Marbles.

Weather, human damage, and the removal of the Elgin Marbles left the Parthenon as an almost empty shell. In the 1820s, Greece won its independence from the Ottoman Empire. In the 1830s, the Greek government moved to protect many of its treasures, including the Parthenon. It removed later additions to the Acropolis and began preserving the original buildings.

A MODERN WONDER

In modern times, the greatest threat to the ancient buildings is air pollution from cars and factories in Athens. Another threat is tourism. More than three million people visit the Acropolis each year. It is one of the modern world's most popular tourist attractions.

Tourists can walk past the Parthenon and other buildings. They can take pictures. However, tourists are not permitted to go inside the buildings. The site is carefully controlled as a historic district.

In 1987 UNESCO named it a World Heritage Site. The Greek government continues to work on restoring the Parthenon and other buildings. Beginning in late 2007, sculptures and other artifacts were moved to the new Acropolis Museum, where they will be restored and protected. The Greek government also continues efforts to get the Elgin Marbles returned from England to Athens.

This book illustration from the 1880s shows the citizens of Athens engaging in public discussion during the time of Pericles (400s B.C.). This is known as the Golden Age of the ancient Greek city.

*H*AVE YOU EVER HEARD PEOPLE MENTION A GOLDEN AGE? IT MEANS A TIME WHEN THE BEST OF THE BEST HAPPENED, WHEN SOMETHING REACHED ITS PEAK. THE GOLDEN AGE FOR A COUNTRY OR A CIVILIZATION USUALLY IS A TIME OF GREAT PEACE AND HAPPINESS, WHEN PEOPLE ENJOY UNUSUALLY GOOD LIVING CONDITIONS.

During the 400s B.C., the city of Athens was one of the most amazing places on Earth. Culture in Athens rose to such a high point that historians decided to call this period the Golden Age of Athens.

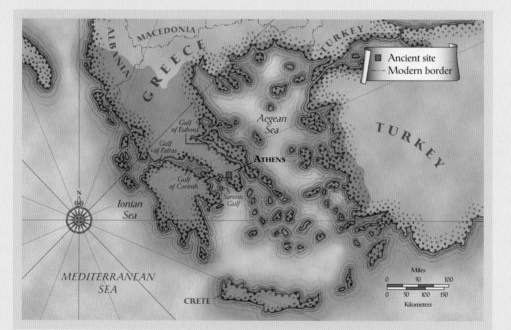

This photo from 1870 shows the ruins on the Acropolis in Athens. Buildings on the Acropolis were designed during the Golden Age of Athens.

In the Golden Age, sculptors in Athens carved beautiful marble statues. These became some of the greatest treasures in modern museums. Architects designed fantastic buildings, such as the Parthenon. Great thinkers, including philosophers and writers, lived in Athens around this time. We still study and use their ideas about government, freedom, and life. Modern movies, TV shows, and other stories are sometimes based on their ideas.

MONEY FOR MARVELS

At this time in history, Greece was not a unified country where people had a national government and obeyed the same laws. Instead, Greek city-states sometimes joined together into "leagues," or alliances, led by one particularly powerful city-state.

Athens was a city-state that controlled a large region called Attika. In 477 B.C., Athens organized an alliance called the Delian League. Its headquarters and treasury were on the island of Delos off the coast of Greece. That group of city-states banded together to fight a long war with the Persian Empire.

After the Delian League defeated the Persians, Athens became the capital of an empire that included all of the Delian League's members. The league's treasury was moved to the Parthenon in Athens.

In the 450s B.C., Pericles (CA. 495–429 B.C.) came to power in Athens. Pericles became a great leader. He had a great ability to make speeches that convinced other government leaders and the people to follow his ideas. Pericles used money from the Delian League to build the Parthenon. He also rebuilt the city of Athens, which had been severely damaged in the Persian War.

Pericles rebuilt the city of Athens when he was in power. This bust of Pericles is a copy of the Greek original and was done by Romans in the second century A.D.

ART AND LEARNING

Athens's wealth drew educated and talented people from all over Greece. Some of the world's greatest artists, writers, and thinkers lived in Athens during the Golden Age. They included the writers Simonides (ca. 556–468 B.C.), Aeschylus (ca. 525–456 B.C.), Sophocles (ca. 496–406 B.C.), Euripides (ca. 480–406 B.C.), and Aristophanes (ca. 448–385 B.C.). Athens was also home to historians Herodotus and Thucydides and the philosopher Socrates (469–399 B.C.).

Athenians loved going to the theater, and many great Golden Age writers wrote plays. Some of these plays were comedies, with humorous scenes, comic characters, and a happy ending. Aristophanes is known as the father of comic drama. Others were tragedies, about unhappy events that made the audience sad or made them think. Aeschylus, Sophocles, and Euripides are Greece's greatest tragedians.

Greek philosophers thought about and discussed many ideas, from the meaning of life to how a government should work. The word *philosophy* comes from Greek words meaning "lover of wisdom." Many historians call Socrates the founder of Western philosophy. Socrates discussed his ideas with many important Athenians. He also taught his ideas and his way of learning to young Athenian men.

DEMOCRACY FOR MEN ONLY

Athens in the Golden Age is also known for its democratic rule. Democracy is often called government by the people. In a democracy, the majority of citizens or their elected representatives make decisions. Pericles encouraged democracy in Athens. He convinced other leaders to allow ordinary citizens to serve in the assembly and have their say in government decisions. Pericles believed that democracy was the best form of government. He encouraged other Greek city-states to become democratic.

A CUP OF *Hemlock*

In modern times, Socrates *(below)* is known as one of history's greatest thinkers. He has influenced many areas of study. But in his own day, Socrates' views got him into trouble. He criticized the Athenian government and leaders. In 399 B.C., Socrates was brought to trial. His accusers said that his teachings were corrupting, or leading astray, the youth of Athens. Socrates was given a choice—leave Athens forever or be put to death. Socrates could not bear leaving his home city. So instead, he drank a cup of hemlock, a deadly poison.

> *"Our form of government is called a democracy because its administration is in the hands, not of a few, but of the whole people."*
>
> —Pericles, leader of Athens, writing in ca. 430 B.C.

But not everyone in Athens got to take part in the democracy. Women, for example, could not vote or take part in government decisions. Neither could the city's slaves, who made up almost one-third of the population of 300,000. Many of these men and women had been captured in wars or born to parents who were slaves. Some slaves worked in pleasant conditions as teachers or servants in rich households. Many, however, had the hardest, dirtiest, and most unpleasant jobs in the city.

This 1882 woodcut shows women in ancient Greece sewing, spinning, and doing other chores. Athenian women were responsible for running households, but they were not allowed to vote during the Golden Age.

PEOPLE RULE

The word *democracy* comes from the Greek words *demos* (people) and *kratos* (rule). Ancient Greece was the first civilization to put democracy into action.

> *"[P]eople in good health were all of a sudden attacked by violent heats in the head, and redness and inflammation in the eyes, the inward parts, such as the throat or tongue, becoming bloody and emitting an unnatural and fetid [rotten] breath."*
>
> —Thucydides (460–400 B.C.), describing a fatal outbreak of disease that helped end the Golden Age of Athens

The Golden Age of Athens ended with the outbreak of the Peloponnesian War between Athens and Sparta (another city-state) in 431 B.C. The war forced Athens to spend its money on armies and weapons, rather than culture. Disease also helped to end the Golden Age. In 430 B.C., a mysterious epidemic began in Athens. It killed about one in every three people, including Pericles and other great leaders. Athens finally surrendered to Sparta in 404 B.C., and the Spartans took control of Athens.

THE LEGACY

The Golden Age in Athens ended, but its legacy continued. For example, one of Socrates' students, Plato (ca. 428–347 B.C.), founded the first European university.

Plato was born to a wealthy, political Athens family. Plato became a student

Men are shown debating in an outdoor court in ancient Athens. This illustration is from the 1889 book History of Civilization *by E. A. Allen.*

of Socrates and adopted Socrates' style of teaching. In 385 B.C., Plato founded a school in Athens. He began teaching young men in an olive grove outside the city walls of Athens. The grove was owned by a man named Academus. Plato's school thus became known as the Academy. At the Academy, students learned philosophy, astronomy, biology, mathematics, and politics.

Aristotle was one of Plato's best students at the Academy. In 335 he founded his own school, the Lyceum. Socrates, Plato, and Aristotle are considered ancient Greece's greatest philosophers.

ANSWERING QUESTIONS *with Questions*

Modern teachers sometimes help students to learn in a way that began in Athens during the Golden Age. Called the Socratic method, it involves teaching by asking questions. It was named after Socrates, who used the method when he was a teacher. The Socratic method begins with a teacher asking the class a question. When students answer, the teacher asks another question. By answering questions with questions, the teacher helps students understand how to think logically. The questions lead students toward the right answer.

These marble busts of Plato (right) and Aristotle (left) were made by sculptors in ancient Rome. The Romans greatly admired Golden Age Athens. Both of the busts are at the Museo Capitolino in Rome, Italy.

Tourists walk around the ruins of the Parthenon in Athens. People come from all over the world to see Greece's ancient wonders.

Greek drama and literature has also had a lasting effect. Greek ideas about how to structure plays, what motivates characters, and how to present certain events influenced many writers throughout the world. In modern times, Greek influence can still be seen in theaters, movies, and TV shows.

A MODERN WONDER

People can see many of the wonders of the Golden Age by visiting modern Athens. More than four million tourists come to this city every year to relive those glorious days of the past. They visit the ruins of actual buildings and monuments from the Golden Age. Tourists also marvel at statues, golden jewelry, and other objects displayed in Athens's museums.

Athens is also one of the few wonders of the world that modern people can enjoy without traveling anywhere. Works of the Golden Age's great writers and thinkers are in libraries, bookstores, museums, and art galleries around the world.

Diners at an outdoor café enjoy a view of the Acropolis in Athens. Millions of tourists come to the city every year to visit the ruins of the Golden Age of Athens.

TIMELINE

CA. 2900 B.C.	The Minoan civilization begins on the island of Crete off the coast of Greece.
1700	Minoans begin building the palace at Knossos on Crete.
1400s	Minoan civilization begins to decline.
1450	The Mycenaean civilization from mainland Greece takes over Crete.
1200s	Mycenae is ruled by the royal family called the Atreids.
1100	Most city-states on the Greek mainland, including Mycenae, are in decline or destroyed. Ancient Greece's dark age begins.
800s	Greece begins to emerge from the dark age. The Greek poet Homer tells the legendary history of Agamemnon and the Trojan War in *The Iliad*.
CA. 800	Greek priests begin building a shrine to Apollo at Delphi.
776	The ancient Olympic Games start in Olympia.
700s	The sanctuary at Epidaurus opens as a medical and religious center.
546	King Croesus of Lydia attacks Persian forces in Asia Minor after consulting the oracle at Delphi.
500s	Athenians begin building temples on the Acropolis.
480s	The Acropolis temples are destroyed during a war between Athens and Persia. Greeks rebuild the temples within sixty years.
477	Athens organizes the Delian League. The city becomes the capital of the Greek Empire.
CA. 456	The Temple of Zeus at Olympia is completed.
450s	Pericles comes to power in Athens. The city's Golden Age begins.
447	Work begins on the Parthenon in Athens.
431	The Peloponnesian War begins between Athens and Sparta. Athens's Golden Age declines.
385	Plato founds the Academy in Athens.
300s	The theater at Epidaurus is built.
146	Greece becomes part of the Roman Empire.
A.D. 390	Roman emperor Theodosius closes the shrines to Apollo at Delphi and elsewhere.
426	Theodosius stops the Olympic Games.
1687	Explosions destroy much of the Parthenon during a battle.
1766	English archaeologist Richard Chandler rediscovers Olympia.

1801	The Earl of Elgin removes sculptures from the Parthenon and ships them to the British Museum in London, England.
1829	German archaeologists begin excavating and uncovering Olympia's ancient buildings.
1874	Heinrich Schliemann uncovers the cyclopean walls, royal shaft graves, and beehive treasuries at Mycenae.
1878	Cretan merchant Minos Kalokairinos discovers ancient ruins at Knossos.
1896	The Olympic Games begin again in Athens, Greece.
1900	Sir Arthur Evans discovers the palace ruins at Knossos.
1936	Officials begin lighting the traditional Olympic torch at the Temple of Hera in Olympia.
1987	Delphi and the Parthenon are added to UNESCO's list of World Heritage Sites.
1988	UNESCO places Epidaurus on its list of World Heritage Sites.
1989	UNESCO adds Olympia to its list of World Heritage Sites.
1999	UNESCO names Mycenae as a World Heritage Site.
2007	Sculptures and other artifacts from the Acropolis are moved to a new museum site in Athens.

CHOOSE AN EIGHTH WONDER

Now that you've read about the seven wonders of ancient Greece, do a little research to choose an eighth wonder. Or make a list with your friends and vote to see which wonder is the favorite.

To do your research, look at some of the websites and books listed in the Further Reading and Websites section of this book. Look for places in Greece that
- *have a cool history*
- *were difficult to make at the time or required new technology*
- *were extra big or tall*
- *were hidden from view or unknown to foreigners for many centuries*

You might even try gathering photos and writing your own chapter on the eighth wonder!

GLOSSARY AND PRONUNCIATION GUIDE

acropolis (uh-KRAH-puh-luhs): a hill in a city on which important buildings are located. The Acropolis in Athens is the site of the Parthenon and other temples.

Apollo (uh-PAH-loh): in Greek mythology, the god of prophecy (predicting the future), healing, light, poetry, and music. Apollo was thought to speak through the Oracle at Delphi.

archaeologists: scientists who study buildings, tools, and other remains of ancient civilizations

artifacts: statues, tools, weapons, and other objects remaining from ancient civilizations

Asclepius (uh-SKLEE-pee-us): the Greek god of healing. Asclepius might have also been a real person—a doctor in Greece in the 1200s B.C.

Athena (uh-THEE-nuh): in Greek mythology, the goddess of wisdom and war. Athena is the patron goddess of Athens.

Athens (A-thuhnz): a leading city-state in ancient Greece and the capital of modern Greece

city-state: a region ruled by a powerful city with its own army and laws

civilization: an organized society specific to a place and time and that often has a government, art, culture, and other advancements

culture: the values, knowledge, and way in which a particular group of people lives

cyclopean (sy-kluh-PEE-uhn): made of huge, rough stones. According to ancient Greek legends, cyclopean buildings or walls were built by a race of giants, the cyclopes.

Delphi (DEL-fye): a city in central Greece that in ancient times was home to a famous oracle

democracy: a form of government in which citizens or their elected representatives make decisions

Doric: a plain, simple architectural style used in some Greek temples

Elgin Marbles: statues that Lord Elgin of Great Britain removed from the Parthenon in the early 1800s

Epidaurus (eh-puh-DAWR-uhs): a town in ancient Greece that became famous as a medical center

golden age: a period in a culture when great achievements are made in art, science, and other areas

Knossos (NOH-sus): a town and palace on the island of Crete and the center of Minoan (muh-NOH-uhn) civilization

labyrinth (LA-buh-rinth): a maze of passageways and walls

Minotaur (MIH-nuh-tawr): in Greek myth, a monster that is half human and half bull

Mycenae (my-SEE-nee): the city at the center of the Mycenaean (my-suh-NEE-uhn) civilization, the first great civilization on the Greek mainland

Nike (NY-kee): in Greek myth, the winged goddess of victory

Olympia (uh-LIM-pee-uh): a town in Greece where the Olympic Games began about 775 B.C.

oracle (OR-uh-kuhl): a person believed to speak for the gods when giving advice about the future. The word *oracle* may also refer to the place such a person can be found.

Parthenon (PAHR-thuh-nahn): a temple to Athena located on the Acropolis in Athens

Pericles (PEHR-uh-kleez): a leader of Athens who lived from about 495 to 429 B.C.

Pythia (PIH-thee-uh): the women who served as oracles at Delphi

Socrates (SAH-kruh-teez): a Greek philosopher and teacher who lived in Athens from about 469 to 399 B.C. Socrates, Plato (PLAY-toh), and Aristotle (A-ruh-STAH-tuhl) are known as ancient Greece's greatest thinkers.

Zeus (ZOOS): in Greek myth, the king of the gods

SOURCE NOTES

8   Homer, *The Odyssey*, trans. Richmond Lattimore (1962; repr. New York: HarperCollins, 1999), 286.

16   Paul Halsall, ed., "Pausanias: Description of Greece, Book II: Corinth," *Internet Ancient History Sourcebook*, 2002, http://www.fordham.edu/halsall/ancient/pausanias-bk2.html (May 8, 2007).

20   Spencer P. M. Harrington, "Behind the Mask of Agamemnon," *Archaeology* 52, no. 4, July–August 1999, http://www.archaeology.org/9907/etc/mask.html (March 12, 2008).

26   Apollodorus, quoted in Emma J. Edelstein and Ludwig Edelstein, *Asclepius: Collection and Interpretation of the Testimonies* (1945; repr. Baltimore: Johns Hopkins Press, 1998), 23.

35   Plutarch, *Moralia*, available online at http://penelope.uchicago.edu/Thayer/E/Roman/Texts/Plutarch/Moralia/De_defectu_oraculorum*.html (March 12, 2008).

45   Lucian of Samosata, *Works*, trans. H. W. Fowler and F. G. Fowler (Oxford, UK: Clarendon Press, 1905), 196.

48   Pausanias, *Description of Greece*, available online at http://www.perseus.tufts.edu/cgi-bin/ptext?doc=Perseus%3Atext%3A1999.01.0160 (March 12, 2007).

55   Pausanias, *Description of Greece*.

58   Evan Hadingham, "Unlocking the Mysteries of the Parthenon," *Smithsonian*, February 2008, 38.

65   Pericles, "Excerpt from Funeral Speech for Athenian War Dead," *The Golden Age of Athenian Democracy under Pericles*, n.d., http://www.rjgeib.com/thoughts/athens/athens.html (May 21, 2007).

66   Thucydides, *The History of the Peloponnesian War*, bk. 2 2000, trans. Richard Crawley, http://classics.mit.edu/Thucydides/pelopwar.2.second.html (April 20, 2007).

SELECTED BIBLIOGRAPHY

Bahn, Paul G., ed. *The Cambridge Illustrated History of Archaeology.* Cambridge: Cambridge University Press, 1999.

Boardman, John, Jasper Griffin, and Oswyn Murray, eds. *The Oxford History of the Classical World.* Oxford: Oxford University Press, 1986.

Bruno, Vincent J., ed. *The Parthenon.* New York: W. W. Norton & Company, 1996.

Hadingham, Evan. "Unlocking the Mysteries of the Parthenon." *Smithsonian,* February 2008, 36–43.

MacKendrick, Paul. *The Greek Stones Speak: The Story of Archaeology in Greek Lands.* New York: W. W. Norton & Company, 1981.

Martin, Thomas R. *Ancient Greece: From Prehistoric to Hellenistic Times.* New Haven, CT: Yale University Press, 1996.

Scarre, Chris, ed. *The Seventy Wonders of the Ancient World: The Great Monuments and How They Were Built.* London: Thames & Hudson, 2000.

Stefoff, Rebecca. *Finding the Lost Cities.* New York: Oxford University Press, 1997.

World Heritage: Archaeological Sites and Urban Centres UNESCO World Heritage. Milan: Skira Editore, 2002.

FURTHER READING AND WEBSITES

Books

Day, Nancy. *Your Travel Guide to Ancient Greece.* Minneapolis: Twenty-First Century Books, 2001. Get your passport to history ready for a trip back to ancient Greece. Learn about local customs, food, famous sites, and much more.

Kotapish, Dawn. *Daily Life in Ancient and Modern Athens.* Minneapolis: Lerner Publications Company, 2001. What did people in ancient Athens eat? What games did kids play? How did people make their living? Kotapish's book looks at how daily life through history has shaped Athens.

Lassieur, Allison. *The Ancient Greeks.* New York: Scholastic, 2004. Lassieur provides a very complete overview of life in ancient Greece. It includes an explanation of why archaeologists are so interested in learning about the ancient Greek civilization.

Lawrence, Caroline. *The Fugitive from Corinth.* New Milford, CT: Roaring Brook Press, 2005. The tenth book in the Roman Mystery series takes readers on an adventure to ancient Greece. Flavia Gemina and her friends travel to Delphi and Athens to track down the person who attacked Flavia's father.

Limke, Jeff. *Theseus: Battling the Minotaur.* Illustrated by John McCrea. Minneapolis: Graphic Universe, 2008. This exciting graphic novel tells the story of the Athenian hero Theseus and his triumph over the monstrous Minotaur.

Pearson, Anne. *Eyewitness Books: Ancient Greece*. New York: DK Publishing, 2004. This Eyewitness Book provides a comprehensive overview of Greek civilization. It explains the economy, religions and myths, culture, and philosophy of the people of ancient Greece.

Woff, Richard. *The Ancient Greek Olympics*. New York: Oxford University Press, 2000. This is a quick read about the ancient Olympic Games. Woff gives an explanation of the religious and athletic events and how they differed from modern Olympic events.

Woods, Michael, and Mary B. Woods. *Ancient Construction: From Tents to Towers*. Minneapolis: Twenty-First Century Books, 2000. Find out about the construction techniques used by the ancient Greeks in the building of the Parthenon. There is also an explanation of the different styles of Greek columns—the Doric, the Ionic, and the Corinthian.

Websites

The Ancient Greek World
http://www.museum.upenn.edu/Greek_World/Index.html
The links at this site from the University of Pennsylvania Museum of Archaeology and Anthropology provides a wealth of information about ancient Greece. It includes information on daily life, religion, and the economy.

The British Museum: Ancient Greece
http://www.ancientgreece.co.uk/
One of the best online sources for ancient Greece, this site is from the British Museum, home of the Elgin Marbles and other treasures. It provides a broad overview of life in ancient Greece.

Greece: Secrets of the Past
http://www.civilisations.ca/civil/greece/gr0000e.html
Get ready for a fascinating trip through ancient Greek history at this Canadian Museum of Civilization site. The museum provides online displays of everything Greek and includes a timeline and links.

Greek Medicine
http://www.nlm.nih.gov/hmd/greek/greek_asclepius.html
This National Library of Medicine site on the history of medicine helps you discover all about the famous Greek healer Asclepius. It also includes the Hippocratic oath that many modern doctors still say when they receive their degrees.

World Heritage List
http://whc.unesco.org/en/list/
Organized by countries, UNESCO's World Heritage List includes natural and historic sites. Each site's page includes a map, a description of the site, a photo gallery, and a list of dangers threatening the site.

INDEX

ABOUT THE AUTHORS

Michael Woods is a science and medical journalist in Washington, D.C., who has won many national writing awards. Mary B. Woods is a school librarian. Their previous books include the eight-volume Ancient Technology series, the Disasters Up Close series, *The History of Communication, The History of Medicine,* and *The Tomb of King Tutankhamen.* The Woodses have four children. When not writing, reading, or enjoying their grandchildren, the Woodses travel to gather material for future books.

PHOTO ACKNOWLEDGMENTS